ELEVATE

THE ESSENCE OF
ZEN

GET BACK TO BASICS

Published by Hinkler Books Pty Ltd
45–55 Fairchild Street
Heatherton Victoria 3202 Australia
www.hinkler.com

hinkler

Author: Mark Levon Byrne
Internal design: Lisa Robertson
Cover design: Maria Daley

Images © Shutterstock.com

ISBN: 978 1 4889 2211 4

Printed and bound in Malaysia

THE ESSENCE OF
ZEN

GET BACK TO BASICS

Mark Levon Byrne

hinkler

CONTENTS

Introduction

Once the name of a Buddhist sect barely known outside Japan, over the last fifty years Zen has spread to the Western world, becoming so widely known and accepted that one can now find 'Zen' body therapies, restaurants, even shampoos.

So what is Zen? There are two ways to answer this question. One is to look at its historical roots in Buddhism and its flowering in medieval Japan. From this point of view, Zen is a Buddhist sect that uses particular meditation and mental practices to end suffering and achieve enlightenment in this lifetime. While these beliefs and practices can be adopted by Westerners, they make little sense outside the context of regular sitting meditation (*zazen*) in the company of other devotees and under the guidance of a master.

Another way to look at Zen is to see it as a distillation of the wisdom of Buddhism into its purest form – an insight into the nature of reality that cannot be communicated by rational thought. Zen leads the mind away from the mind, until the spark of direct insight appears in a simple brush stroke, a rippling brook or a hearty laugh. From this perspective, we are living a Zen life whenever we are wholly in the present, without our usual fears, hopes and distractions. Meditation might reveal this life to us, but equally, we might find it in any other activity, if it is done with the right attitude.

These two ways of understanding might be called 'formal Zen' and 'broad Zen'. This book pays equal respect to both approaches. It explores the historical roots of Zen, how it relates to Buddhist teachings, and how it is practised today, both in Japan and the West. It also looks at Zen in non-traditional contexts, such as politics and psychotherapy, and will take you on a quest for the elusive but tantalising 'essence of Zen'.

If Zen does have an essence, it is to be found not by uncovering an absolute truth hidden to outsiders, but by adopting an attitude to life that is at once playful and disciplined, sophisticated and utterly simple, steeped in tradition and yet completely spontaneous. Such paradoxes are central to Zen: the Zen student strives for enlightenment, but to become enlightened one must give up all striving.

To further complicate matters, no eternal Self exists to enlighten anyway. On the other hand, we all possess Buddha-nature, so we are all enlightened already!

How to find a way through this minefield? Ultimately, this is a task for each of us to work on in our own lives. I hope this book will provide some clues, and will inform, inspire, delight and challenge you along the way.

The Buddhist heritage

The Indian background

The India into which the Buddha was born over 2,500 years ago was a land of great intellectual and religious activity. It was in transition between a tribal society with a religious life based around the worship of local nature spirits and gods, and the newer religion of the Vedas and the Upanishads, brought to India by semi-nomadic horsemen and cattle herders from the north, which combined elaborate sacrifices with subtle philosophical speculation. (These are the same Indo-Europeans who travelled west to Europe and became the ancestors of most modern European peoples.)

Several beliefs central to Hinduism became important to Buddhism:

- *Brahman*, a single cosmic power that is embodied in human form in the pure or eternal Self, the *Atman*.
- *Samsara*, the cycle of birth and death that repeats until the soul attains liberation, *moksha*. One can attain liberation by following moral codes called *dharmas* and by performing spiritual practices and rituals called yogas. The more extreme ascetic practices were (and still are) undertaken by wandering, often naked holy men called *sadhus*, who tortured their bodies and endured great privations to attain liberation from the wheel of birth and death.
- Karma, meaning 'action'; every act or thought has consequences, creating a store of 'good' or 'bad' karma that influences whether one is reborn as a human or as a lower life form.
- The caste system, which applies the doctrine of karma to human society, so that a high-caste Brahman is thought more pure and holy than an 'untouchable' *Harijan*. Only a Brahman can officiate at religious rituals and attain liberation, and movement between the castes is not possible during one's lifetime.

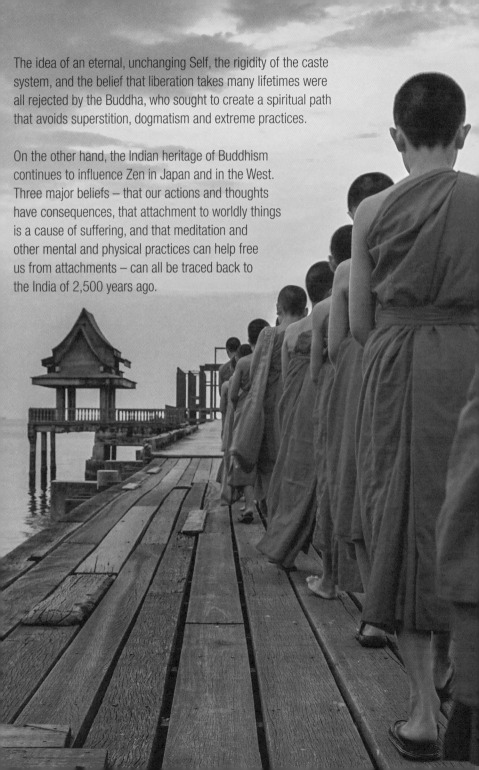

The idea of an eternal, unchanging Self, the rigidity of the caste system, and the belief that liberation takes many lifetimes were all rejected by the Buddha, who sought to create a spiritual path that avoids superstition, dogmatism and extreme practices.

On the other hand, the Indian heritage of Buddhism continues to influence Zen in Japan and in the West. Three major beliefs – that our actions and thoughts have consequences, that attachment to worldly things is a cause of suffering, and that meditation and other mental and physical practices can help free us from attachments – can all be traced back to the India of 2,500 years ago.

The life of the Buddha

Believe nothing, no matter where you read it or who has said it,
not even if I have said it, unless it agrees with your own reason and
your own common sense.
— attributed to the Buddha

The Buddha, the 'awakened one', was born Siddhartha (meaning 'goal accomplished') Gautama, a prince of the hill tribe of the Sakyas in northern India, in the sixth century BC. After being indulged as a child, he rejected his royal upbringing and studied with various teachers, living the life of an ascetic before rejecting it in favour of what he would come to call the 'middle way'. He began to proclaim his own teachings after he achieved enlightenment, and soon attracted followers.

Around this core of historical fact has grown up a great deal of legend. Stories abound concerning the Buddha's previous lives, his birth and childhood, his time as an ascetic and his life as a teacher.

The most famous tale relates how he came to leave the palace and become a wandering ascetic. Having lived his life within the palace walls, Siddhartha as a young man expressed a desire to tour the city in which he lived. His father reluctantly consented, but arranged (as is done for many modern politicians) for Siddhartha's route to be brightly decorated and full of cheering crowds. In spite of these precautions, Siddhartha saw in turn a sick man, an old man and a funeral ceremony. Having been exposed to the reality of suffering and the impermanence of life, he could not go back to his life of luxury; he left his wife and child one night, as they slept, to become a sadhu.

After about five years of increasingly harsh self-discipline, he was sleeping on thorns and eating only a handful of rice a day. However, this only weakened his body and made it difficult to concentrate, so one day he accepted a bowl of milk rice from a local girl. Rejected by his fellow sadhus for what they saw as his surrender to temptation, Siddhartha then began his quest to find a middle way between the extremes of indulgence and denial.

Sitting under a sacred *bodhi* ('knowledge') or pipal tree in Bodhgaya one day, he vowed not to move from that spot until he became enlightened. As night fell, thoughts of his previous life of luxury crowded his mind, and he was tempted to return to the palace. These thoughts passed, and next he recalled in detail all his previous lives. He did battle in his mind with the forces of evil personified by Mara, the god of desire or the demon of illusion, and pointed to the earth as his witness that he was worthy of becoming a buddha. In the last hours before dawn, Siddhartha realised the doctrine of *pratitya samutpada*, the interdependence of all things. This became the basis of the Four Noble Truths, the central teaching of Buddhism.

The newly awakened Buddha sat for seven days in a state of bliss. He then set out to find his former colleagues. He found them in the deer park at Sarnath, near Benares (modern Varanasi). At first, they resolved to ignore him, but his radiance made that impossible, and they became his first followers. There he taught his first sutra or sermon, known as the 'sermon setting in motion the wheel of the truth', which explained the Four Noble Truths and the Eightfold Path to end suffering.

Over the next 45 years, the Buddha accepted some 500 followers, without regard to their caste or gender. His first followers were male forest hermits and ascetics called *bhikkus*, but after accepting that women, too, could attain enlightenment (in contrast to Hindu teaching, which required them to be reborn as men first), he accepted female *bhikkus* or *bhikkunis* as well. Thus was born the first *sangha*, or monastic community.

At the age of eighty, the Buddha announced his impending death to his cousin Ananda, head of the sangha. Suffering food poisoning, he rested on his side in the state of *parinirvana*, the state of complete liberation from which return to earthly life is impossible. His last words were said to be:

All things are impermanent. Work on your salvation with diligence.

Resolutely train yourself to attain peace.

Buddha

The basic principles of Buddhism

All Buddhist doctrines and practices stem from the first sermon preached by the Buddha in the Deer Park at Sarnath. The first and second Noble Truths constitute a psychological diagnosis of suffering (*dukkha*), which the Buddha regarded as being caused by our desires (*tanha*): for things, for permanence and control, even for love. The Eightfold Path is his prescription for ending suffering. It combines knowledge of basic doctrines (1 and 2) with the appropriate moral outlook (3 to 6) – for instance, 'right vocation', which prohibits earning a living by any means that would harm other creatures or oneself – and practical means of achieving insight through meditation (7 and 8). Several important beliefs underlie the Four Noble Truths and the Eightfold Path:

- All existence is *anicca*, impermanent, so the desire for things to stay the same is a source of suffering.
- *Anatman*: because things are constantly changing, there can be no eternal, unchanging Self or *Atman*.
- Instead, existence is characterised by *sunyata*, emptiness. This means related to everything else, rather than void. This is the doctrine of *pratitya samutpada*, or 'interdependent origination'.
- Attaining *nirvana*, enlightenment, depends not on the worship of a god or the performance of particular rituals but on individual effort.

It is easy to reject the Buddha's diagnosis of our ills and his prescription for healing them as irrelevant and pessimistic. Certainly, life was much less predictable and materially secure in India 2,500 years ago (and even today) than it is for those of us lucky enough to live in the modern West. But our lives are still subject to change – perhaps more than ever before, and much of it out of our control. Look at the things we collect: how happy do they really make us, or do we have to keep on and on acquiring, and working ever harder to afford all the things we think we need? To acknowledge that our desires to have things stay the same and to control our lives cause us suffering, and that a life of deep satisfaction and meaning does not come without effort – these are 'noble truths' even today.

What is nirvana?

Literally, nirvana means 'cooled' or 'quenched', as in the 'blowing out of a flame'. This is the flame of samsara, the cycle of birth and death. It suggests that Buddhism is a nihilistic religion that wants its followers to escape from the world into nothingness. However, for most Buddhists, it is attachment to the world of samsara that is destructive, not life or consciousness as a whole.

Buddhas and bodhisattvas

A buddha is one who has attained enlightenment by his or her own efforts. An *arhat* (or arhant) has attained the same goal with the help of a teacher. A bodhisattva is also enlightened, but instead of leaving the world as a buddha does, a bodhisattva chooses to stay here to work for the enlightenment of all other sentient beings. This raises an interesting problem. If a buddha chooses to leave the world rather than work for the salvation of others, is he or she really enlightened?

Apart from the historical Buddha, there are said to be various past and future buddhas and bodhisattvas. These include:

- **AVALOKITESHVARA** (*Kuan-Yin* in China, *Kannon* in Japan), 'the Lord who Looks Down', the bodhisattva of compassion.
- **MAITREYA**, the future Buddha, who appears in order to revive the Buddha's teaching at a time when it has disappeared.
- **AMITABHA** (*Amida* in Japan), 'Immeasurable Radiance', who dwells in the heaven of the west.

Early Buddhism

Not long after the Buddha's death, some 500 of his followers met for the Council of Rajagaha. There, they agreed on what the Buddha had said. These teachings, which were not written down until about 100 BC, became known as the Sutta Pitaka, or Sermon Collection, and constitute the middle part of the Buddhist canon known as the Tripitaka, or 'Three Baskets'. The other 'baskets' are the *Vinaya* (Conduct) and the *Abhidhamma* (Supplementary Doctrines).

A second Council was held about a century later, to resolve differences about how strictly the rules agreed on at the first Council for the behaviour of monks should be enforced. Conservatives won the day, with the result that a group called the Mahasanghikas broke away. The Mahasanghikas also disagreed about the goal of Buddhist practice. They believed that the arhat was a less worthy ideal than the bodhisattva.

> No snowflake ever falls in the wrong place.

Zen proverb

This split would eventually see the Buddhist world divided into two main branches. The southern, Theravada branch is now found in Sri Lanka, Thailand and Indochina, and prides itself on having stayed close to the Buddha's own teachings. It is humanistic rather than spiritual, and practical and devotional rather than mystical. Its adherents place great emphasis on the storing up of merit by the performance of good deeds (such as alms-giving, donating to temples, and following the Eightfold Path) in order to ensure a better rebirth.

The northern, *Mahayana* ('Greater Vehicle') tradition is found in China, Vietnam, Korea and Japan. Mahayana sees itself as representing the spirit, rather than the word, of the Buddha's message. Apart from its less rigid adherence to the precepts for monks and its championing of the bodhisattva ideal, it also started a process of spiritualising the Buddha. Where Theravadans regard him as an ordinary man who became enlightened through his own efforts, Mahayanans believe that he had *trikaya*, 'three bodies': a *dharmakaya*, or eternal essence; a *sambogakaya* that is apparent only to other buddhas and bodhisattvas; and a *rupakaya*, or *nirmanakaya*, his human manifestation. Thus, in one sense he was always enlightened. This idea was later extended to the belief that all beings possess an essential Buddha-nature, which is only waiting to be revealed.

Tibetan Buddhists regard their tradition, known as *Vajrayana*, the 'Diamond Vehicle', as a further development of Mahayana teachings. Vajrayana places more emphasis on the elaborate ritual and meditative use of *mantras* (devotional chants), *mudras* (hand gestures) and *mandalas* (circular symbolic representations of the cosmos). It also emphasises the role of the teacher as guru, and his or her place in a lineage (a line of teachers) going right back to the Buddha.

The Sixth Patriarch

Hui-neng was regarded as an ignorant barbarian when he arrived at Hung-jen's monastery, and so was put to work pounding rice in the kitchen. He had been there eight months when the Fifth Patriarch called the monks together and told them he would pass on his robe of authority to whoever could come up with a verse that revealed deep understanding of the dharma. In the dead of night, the senior monk wrote the following verse on a wall:

Our body is the tree of perfect wisdom, / And our mind is a bright mirror.
At all times diligently wipe them, /So that they will be free from dust.

While competent, it was an orthodox and unimaginative attempt, and Hung-jen told him to go away and try again in a couple of days. Meanwhile, Hui-neng secretly wrote the following verse on the wall:

The tree of perfect wisdom is originally no tree.
/ Nor has the bright mirror any frame.
Buddha-nature is forever clear and pure. / Where is there any dust?

Hung-jen proclaimed it not good enough, but at midnight called Hui-neng to come to him. He expounded the Diamond Sutra, which the young 'barbarian' understood at once. The Fifth Patriarch then proclaimed Hui-neng his successor, gave him the robe signifying the office of patriarch, and advised him to leave at once to avoid being killed by other jealous monks. When things had settled down at the monastery, Hui-neng returned to take his place as the Sixth Patriarch.

Ch'an: Chinese Zen

Buddhism spread to China via Central Asia and eastern Iran around the first century AD. It encountered considerable resistance, however, from followers of Confucianism and Taoism. In order to be accepted in China, Buddhism had to become more practical and lose much of its otherworldliness.

Especially after the pilgrimage of the Chinese monk Fa-Hsien to India in AD 399–413, two-way contact between Chinese and Indian Buddhists resulted in the introduction of many Mahayana sutras, the widespread acceptance of Buddhist teachings by the aristocracy and ordinary people, and the development of a number of distinctive Chinese schools of Buddhism.

The most popular was *Ching-t'u*, or Pure Land, which used a simple devotional practice involving recitation of the name of the Buddha Amitabha to bring about rebirth in the Western paradise. But the most influential was *Ch'an*. Although based on meditation practices dating back to the first Buddhists in China, Ch'an did not emerge as a distinct school until the time of Hung-jen (died AD 713). Hung-jen traced his lineage back to Bodhidharma, an Indian monk said to have arrived in China around AD 520. However, the original Ch'an Buddhist was supposed to have been the Indian monk Kasyapa. The Ch'an school soon developed a large body of literature about the lives and teachings of its patriarchs, and gained a reputation for rejecting pomp and pretension in favour of direct insight. It reached its finest flowering in the Platform Sutra of the Sixth Patriarch, Hui-neng.

One other Ch'an master has had a lasting influence on Zen. Pai-chang (died AD 814) developed a monastic rule based on a new precept: 'A day without work is a day without food.' As well as ensuring that Ch'an monks would not be a burden on the general populace, this precept reflected the Ch'an belief that enlightenment is not a matter only for the meditation hall, but can be found in everyday life. Other Ch'an masters during the T'ang period (AD 618–906) introduced the shouts, slaps and paradoxical *koans* (riddles or short dialogues) familiar to modern students of Zen.

In the ninth century, Chinese Buddhists suffered severe persecution as proponents of a foreign religion. Ch'an survived because it had never been associated with great wealth or power, and so was not perceived as a threat. It continued to have only a minor place in the religious life of China, but even today many Chinese believe in the essential harmony of their three religious traditions. In the meantime, Ch'an migrated to Korea, Vietnam and Japan.

Dhyana/Ch'an/Zen

The Chinese character Ch'an (Zen in Japanese) is derived from the Sanskrit term dhyana, meaning contemplation. Ch'an/Zen is composed of two elements. On the left is an altar. On the right are three elements (at the top an owl, symbolising learning; under it a brain and a needle) that, when joined, mean 'simple'. Together, they emphasise the centrepiece of the Zen tradition: sitting meditation.

Kasyapa and the flower

Zen dates its origin to a day when (so the story goes) the Buddha was seated at Vulture Peak. He was offered a flower and asked to teach the dharma. Instead of speaking, he simply held the flower before him and slowly turned it. Alone among the audience, Kasyapa (or Mahakasyapa) smiled, revealing his spontaneous understanding of the Buddha's message.

Bodhidharma

Bodhidharma was a Brahman priest who converted to Buddhism in the late fifth or early sixth centuries AD. He was instructed by his teacher to go on a pilgrimage to China. On arriving, he was summoned to appear before the emperor Wu-ti, an ardent Buddhist.

Emperor: 'How much merit have I accumulated by my support of the dharma?'
Bodhidharma: 'No merit at all.'

Emperor: 'What, then, is the first principle of the dharma?'
Bodhidharma: 'Just emptiness, nothing sacred.'

Emperor: 'Who, then, stands before me?'
Bodhidharma: 'I don't know.'

Bodhidharma was giving the emperor a lesson in true Buddhism, which has nothing to do with 'doing the right thing' or abstract philosophy, but the emperor didn't get it. Unimpressed, the emperor dismissed the impudent foreign monk, who then travelled to the north of China and reputedly spent nine years meditating in a cave, even cutting off his eyelids to prevent himself from falling asleep and letting his legs rot under him.

To escape from the
world means that
one's mind is not
concerned with the
opinions of the world.

Dogen

Japanese Zen

Zen in Japanese history

Just as Buddhism in China had to contend with the native Taoist and Confucian traditions, in Japan it faced *Shinto*, the 'way of the gods'. Shinto revolves around the worship of *kami*, ancestral spirits or gods that dwell in heaven or in the forces of nature. The Japanese emperor is believed to be 'manifest kami', a direct descendant of the Sun Goddess Ameratsu Omikami. Ancestors and living people with special powers are also thought of as kami. Waterfalls, trees, even rocks are places where kami dwell, and are often enclosed by *shimenawa*, sacred ropes. Also characteristic of Shinto are *torii*, the inverted arches that often form the entrance to shrines and are painted red; the huge wooden pillars and thatched roofs of Shinto shrines; and *matsuri*, the seasonal festivals when people come closer to the kami, which are invoked in rituals featuring bonfires and fireworks, drumming and dancing.

In many respects, Shinto is no different today from the way it was in the sixth century AD, when the first Chinese and Korean monks crossed the seas to spread the Buddha's teachings on suffering and enlightenment. Buddhism quickly gained official acceptance, becoming an important ingredient in the constitution that was developed by Prince Shotoku (AD 574–622) to help create a unified state out of a country that was rent by clan divisions. For instance, the second article of the constitution repeats the basic Buddhist precepts in exhorting people to revere the Three Treasures – the Buddha, his teachings (the dharma), and the community of his followers (the sangha).

Among the most influential Buddhist schools in Japan during this early period of assimilation was the *Sanron* ('Three Treatises' or 'Way of Emptiness'), based on early Mahayana teachings on the emptiness of all things. Highly sceptical and philosophical, it was eventually supplanted during the Nara period (AD 708–781) by other schools, including relatives of the Tantric and Pure Land schools that developed in China and other Mahayana countries.

Although Ch'an was introduced into Japan in the Nara period, it remained a minor sect until the Kamakura period (AD 1195–1333), when two famous Japanese monks, Eisai and Dogen, the founders of the Rinzai and Soto schools of Zen, respectively, went to China to study. Eisai incorporated elements of existing schools into his teachings, finding favour with the shogunate (the military rulers) in the new capital of Kamakura (near Tokyo). Dogen spurned other schools and political patronage, and set up the first independent Zen temple in Japan in AD 1236.

Zen's position as the religion of the shogunate was reinforced by the military training (especially in swordsmanship and archery) instituted by Zen monks. This development gave rise to the samurai, the warrior class who used Buddhism for ends undreamt of by their religion's founder, a dedicated pacifist.

After Dogen's death in AD 1253, civil wars and government controls led to Zen gradually losing political favour and cohesiveness, but it was revived in the eighteenth century by Hakuin Ekaku, who reorganised monastic discipline and koan practice.

Today about 2.5 million Rinzai and 7 million Soto Zen followers can be found in Japan. There is also a third sect, Obaku, introduced from China in AD 1654 by the monk Ingen. It combines zazen with the Pure Land practice of reciting the name of the Buddha Amida, and is sometimes called 'Nembutsu (short for the chant "Namu Amida-bu", "Hail to the Buddha Amida") Zen'.

The first buddhas in Japan

In the year AD 522, a Korean ruler sent a request to Japan for military assistance. As Buddhism was already well established in Korea, he sent gifts of Buddhist sutras and a statue of the Buddha. The accompanying message read, 'The new doctrine of the Buddha is exceedingly excellent, although difficult to explain and comprehend.'

The Japanese were wary of allowing a foreign religion to compete with Shinto, but decided to allow the statue to remain for a trial period, to test its magical powers. But soon a pestilence – probably smallpox – decimated the land, and the statue was dumped in a drainage canal.

Twenty years later, the same thing happened under a new emperor, but when the second statue was destroyed, the plague worsened – something the new religion's supporters were able to turn to their advantage. The emperor vacillated about how to respond, so followers of the new religion assassinated him. From then on, the new religion began to take hold.

Central teachings

Zen inherits the central teachings of Mahayana Buddhism:

- *Sunyata* – nothing has a fixed and separate identity, so all things are interdependent.
- All beings possess Buddha-nature – that is, the ability to become enlightened.
- The non-duality of samsara and nirvana – the everyday world and the world of enlightenment are not separate.
- The bodhisattva ideal – wisdom and insight are to be shared for the benefit of all sentient beings.

However, Zen also claims to be unique, featuring:

- A special transmission outside the scriptures.
- No dependence on words and letters.
- Direct pointing to the mind of humankind.
- Seeing into one's nature and the attainment of Buddhahood.

These lines (ascribed to Bodhidharma, but probably written by a later Ch'an teacher) reflect the belief that insight and wisdom are lived experiences that cannot be encapsulated in words. For instance, in the *Lankavatara Sutra*, one of the earliest Mahayana scriptures and an important reference for Zen, it is said that:

... the highest reality is an exalted state of bliss,
and as it cannot be entered into by mere statements regarding it,
words are not the highest reality.
— Lankavatara Sutra

While other schools emphasise the need to believe in a power outside oneself to attain enlightenment, Zen teaches that Buddha-nature is within us all and can be awakened by our own efforts. Whereas enlightenment was a permanent state for earlier Buddhists, in Zen it comes mostly in momentary flashes of insight called *satori*.

Accounts of how Zen masters attained satori are a staple of Zen literature. For one monk, it was just the sound of a pebble as he swept the ground in front of the temple. Hakuin, the father of modern Rinzai Zen, had a breakthrough when he was about to be hit by a madman with a broom, and another when he was walking through knee-high water during heavy rain. Such experiences cannot be predicted, let alone forced, but the ground is laid for them by long periods of zazen and (in Rinzai) koan practice. The most important insight of Zen is not about the nature of enlightenment, or even about the best way to attain it, but about where it is to be found. Satori is not a lofty, transcendental experience; it is a glimpse into the profundity of everyday life. This is celebrated in one of the most famous Zen verses:

How marvellous, how wonderful: I chop wood, I carry water!

Zen has no time for speculation about life after death, other worlds, even mystical states. Zen would agree with Henry David Thoreau, who, when asked about the afterlife, replied, 'One world at a time!' Forget tomorrow and yesterday: what is happening right here, right now? If we give this our full attention – but without attachment, for it and we will change – satori is ours. It is not surprising that the verse above gave rise to another:

Before enlightenment, chop wood, carry water.
After enlightenment, chop wood, carry water.

Five Zen masters

Eisai

Eisai was originally a monk at Mt Hiei near Kyoto, but travelled twice to China to deepen his understanding of the dharma. Finding Ch'an to be the only Buddhist sect still prospering there, he studied at the temple of T'ien-t'ung shan before returning to Japan in AD 1191 as a master of the Rinzai (Lin-chi in Chinese) school. Facing hostility from established sects in the capital, Kyoto, he escaped to Kamakura, where he developed a close relationship with the shoguns. He eventually returned to Kyoto, but was only allowed to promulgate Zen on condition that he grant a place in his teachings to the other, established Buddhist schools. His adaptability and ability to compromise did much to legitimise Zen in medieval Japan.

Dogen

The other great founder of Zen in Japan was the high-born and well-educated Dogen, the descendant of an emperor on one side of his family and a prime minister on the other. Indeed, young Dogen showed such promise that he was being groomed for the prime ministership before he chose the life of a monk. Like Eisai, he studied at Mt Hiei, but was disappointed by what he found there. 'It is taught that "we are all born Buddha",' he later wrote, 'but I have been unable to find among the inmates a single person who looks like a Buddha.'

Dogen had a problem. If all beings are already Buddha, then why practise endlessly? This question bothered him for years. He went to see Eisai shortly before he died, followed in his footsteps to China, stayed at T'ien-t'ung shan for two years, and then travelled to other monasteries in search of a teacher. He was about to return to Japan when he heard Ju-ching, the new abbot of T'ien-t'ung, explain that Zen practice meant 'dropping off both body and mind', and he immediately attained enlightenment. He realised that Buddha-nature is not something we own like a suit, but must be lived from moment to moment, and that meditation is the best way to do this.

Given the seal of the dharma by Ju-ching, he returned to Japan and began to teach Zen. Again like Eisai, he came under pressure to acknowledge the other schools. Unlike Eisai, Dogen refused, and moved to a remote province to continue teaching his brand of Zen, which was later called Soto. The Rinzai school uses the koan as a device to concentrate the mind while meditating. Dogen believed this practice was too directed towards 'obtaining a certain thing'. He preferred the practice of 'just sitting' in meditation (*shikantaza*) as an end in itself. The difference between Rinzai and Soto is often characterised as being between methods of sudden and gradual enlightenment. While koan practice appealed to intellectuals and the idea of sudden, direct enlightenment appealed to the warrior class, the more gentle approach of Soto led to it becoming more popular among the common people.

Ikkyu

Ikkyu (AD 1394–1481) was an illegitimate son of the emperor, who disowned him and rejected his mother. She put him in a monastery at an early age to keep him safe. At the age of sixteen he became the only disciple of an obscure monk called Keno, and was so devastated when Keno died four years later that he tried to drown himself. Thereafter attaching himself to another lit-tle-known monk called Kaso, he practised hard and attained his first glimpse of satori at the age of twenty-four. Afterwards, he wrote:

> *From the world of passions returning to the world of passions:*
> *There is a moment's pause.*
> *If it rains, let it rain; if the wind blows, let it blow.*

He had a deeper experience of satori two years later, prompted by the sound of a crow cawing. Several years later he left Kaso and began a period of wandering that would last thirty years.

He was known for attacking the corrupt Zen establishment and for having women students. He refused to conform to social mores, frequenting bars and brothels, having a son, and possibly being married for a time. He warned people against 'loving the sacred and hating the secular'.

Ikkyu's 'Red Thread Zen' refuses to regard women as corrupting influences on the road to enlightenment, and sees sexual union as a legitimate spiritual practice. At the age of seventy-seven, Ikkyu had a scandalous affair with a much younger blind singer, composer and musician called Nori. He wrote her erotic poems, and incorporated elements of their sexual relationship into his Zen teaching. Despite his lack of conformity with other Zen schools, at the age of eighty he was pressured to become abbot of Daitokuji, and set about rebuilding it after it was nearly destroyed by civil war. The task was completed just before his death at the age of eighty-four.

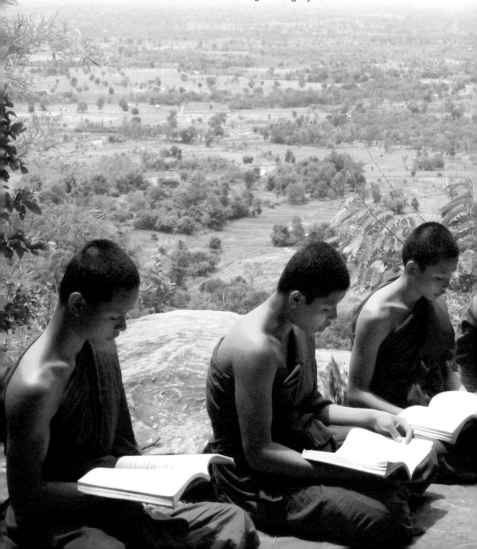

Takuan

Takuan Soho (AD 1573–1645) was trained at the great Rinzai temple of Daitokuji in Kyoto, but was exiled to the north of Japan after protesting against government interference in the temple's affairs. He eventually returned, and was persuaded to travel to Edo (Tokyo) to meet the shogun, who built him a temple, the Tokaiji, to keep him close by. An accomplished swordsman and writer, he left thousands of letters to his followers in simple, accessible Japanese.

Hakuin

By the time of Hakuin (AD 1686–1769), Rinzai Zen, like Japanese Buddhism as a whole, had been corrupted by the worldly ambitions of its monks and the influence of Nembutsu chanting, which required no attempt at personal insight. Hakuin settled in the small, remote temple of Shoinji to devote himself to the revival of pure, serious Zen training, and soon gained followers from all sections of society, from farmers to samurai. An eloquent writer as well as calligrapher and sculptor, he also left an autobiography.

Zen, bushido and politics

Zen owed much of its early success to its close association with the ruling class. This was partly due to the affinity of the shoguns for the austere and disciplined practices of Zen. This led to a strong Zen influence in *bushido*, the 'way of the warrior' practised by samurai, martial arts exponents and kamikaze pilots alike.

Zen teachings on emptiness and no-self allowed a samurai to believe that death (whether his own or his opponent's) is no more real than life. Zen training allowed him to cultivate detachment from his opponent; to calm his mind before battle, eliminating fear and hatred; and to act spontaneously, without thought or regret. His sword or bow then became an extension of his own body and mind, and he could take advantage of his opponent's weaknesses rather than being driven by his own.

The Zen influence on samurai training was institutionalised in response to the threat of invasion from the armies of Kublai Khan between ad 1268 and 1281. The Mongols inspired fear in their enemies, but the samurai, with the help of their Zen training, overcame their fear of death. On the Khan's third attempt to invade, his navy was met by a line of samurai warriors that didn't break in seven weeks of fighting. When the August typhoons struck, the invading navy was decimated, and the soldiers who made it to shore were slaughtered. In honour of the victory, the emperor named the typhoon the Kamikaze or Divine Wind.

The samurai class continued to wield a major influence in Japan until the Meiji Restoration, a period of modernisation forced on the country following the landing of American ships led by Commodore Perry in ad 1853. The samurai were regarded as relics of a feudal past, but with Japanese victories against the Chinese in 1894 and the Russians in 1905, bushido gained a new lease of life. Zen monks and teachers played an active part in this process. For instance, Soyen Shaku, D.T. Suzuki's teacher and the first Zen teacher to travel to the USA, considered opposition to war to be a 'product of egotism', while the great Soto Zen patriarch Sawaki Kodo wrote of him and his fellow soldiers gorging themselves on killing people. In 1992 the Soto sect issued a 'Statement of Repentance' for its wartime activities.

The association of Zen with bushido shows that spiritual teachings can be misused. Rather than being a reason to reject Zen, it might remind us that a complete religious life also involves rational reflection and the exercise of moral judgement.

Zen ethics

Buddhism doesn't recognise most of the common rites of passage (birth, puberty, marriage and death). The only transformation of importance is that from suffering and ignorance to enlightenment. So 'taking refuge' (whether once, or on a daily basis) is as important in Zen as in other schools of Buddhism.

I take refuge in the Buddha. I take refuge in the dharma.
I take refuge in the sangha.

This means devoting oneself to the teacher, following the 'middle way', and becoming part of the community of followers. It has also been interpreted as committing oneself to a life of realisation, truth and harmony.

In daily life, the vows of refuge are reflected in the Three Pure Precepts:

Renounce all evil; practise all good; save the many beings.

In turn, these precepts are reflected in the Ten Grave Precepts that constitute the Buddhist equivalent to the Ten Commandments of Christianity: not killing, not stealing, not misusing sex, not lying, not giving or taking drugs, not discussing faults of others, not praising yourself while abusing others, not sparing the dharma assets, not indulging in anger and not defaming the Three Treasures.

The other foundation of Zen morality is the Bodhisattva Vow, which is common to both the Mahayana and the Vajrayana traditions:

Sentient beings are numberless: we vow to save them all.
Passions are endless: we vow to extinguish them all.
The teachings are infinite: we vow to learn them all.
The Buddha way is inconceivable: we vow to attain it.

But however many precepts one has vowed to uphold, the ethics of Zen are contextual rather than absolute. The Mahayana tradition calls this upaya, 'skillful means'.

You know the sound
of two hands clapping;
tell me, what is the
sound of one hand?

Hakuin

Koan practice

'Does a dog have Buddha-nature?'

'Mu!'

A nonsensical answer to a philosophical question? 'Joshu's Mu' is the first in the great koan collection, the *Mumonkan* ('Gateless Gate'), and is traditionally the first given to Zen students. Buddhist doctrine suggests that the question be answered in the affirmative: all sentient beings have Buddha-nature, so dogs must also. But the answer is 'Mu', which literally means 'no'. There is something else going on here – but what is it?

Koans arose in the Ch'an tradition, as questions and answers between teachers and students. The more interesting and memorable of these became known as *kung-an*, public documents, and were recorded, along with the commentaries of later masters.

The original koan was the Buddha holding up a flower when asked to discourse on the dharma. Koans are intended to use the mind against the mind: to break through normal ways of understanding to a deeper, more intuitive awareness. Rinzai students focus on them in meditation – and in daily life, too, so that one becomes 'like a small terrier clinging to an elephant', as a modern Zen teacher put it. The idea is not to become obsessed with solving the riddle on a mental level but to hold it in the back of one's mind and let it stimulate doubt, like the grain of sand that irritates an oyster into producing a pearl. Huang-po, who is credited with being the founder of the koan tradition, said of 'Mu':

Contemplate this word Mu twenty-four hours a day. Study it from morning to night. Mobilize your energy and hold onto this word 'Mu' continuously from mind moment to mind moment. Whether you are walking, standing, sitting, or lying down; whether you are dressing or eating or going to the toilet, after long days and years you will achieve unity. Unexpectedly the mind flower will bloom and you will awaken to the devices of the buddhas and ancestors. After this you will be able to open your big mouth and say things like, 'Bodhidharma's coming from the west,' thus creating waves with no wind.
— Huang-po

Students are given a koan by their teacher, and present their understanding of it in interviews. It isn't enough to parrot someone else's answer: the response must reveal a genuine understanding that goes beyond words. When the teacher is satisfied, the student is given another koan, in a series that could, if one is given all available koans, take thirty years to complete.

The requirement for direct, often non-verbal insight is why koan practice is often associated with some of the more bizarre (to outsiders) behaviour of Zen teachers. What looks to us like verbal and physical abuse — slapping, nose-twisting, kicking and the like — is not uncommon. In fact, the master Toku-san used to say, 'Thirty blows of my stick when you have something to say: thirty blows just the same when you have nothing to say.' If this seems not just nonsensical but ridiculous, even annoying, then the grain of sand referred to earlier is starting to do its job.

Even more famous in the West than 'Joshu's Mu' is Hakuin's koan, 'What is the sound of one hand clapping?' Even Bart Simpson got the rational answer to this one (you can actually clap one hand!), but the deeper question is, what lies beyond our habitual way of seeing things? Or, what is the essence of things? What is your true nature?

Here are two other well-known koans:

All things return to the one. Where does the one return to?

What is your original face — the one you had before your parents were born?

The life of the Zen monk

In Japan, Zen is practised at local temples which serve as a focus for village worship. Larger temples or monasteries ordain monks and have a training role. Monks and nuns are often married, but they must remain celibate for the three years of training they undertake in a monastery.

Larger temple compounds typically consist of walled gardens with wooden gateways, a Buddha hall (*butsuden*), a dharma hall (*hondo*), a meditation hall (*zendo*), a tea hut and smaller outbuildings. The main statue in the butsuden is usually of the Buddha (often flanked by Bodhidharma), but it may sometimes be of one of the bodhisattvas. The sixteen arhats, who are miracle workers and tamers of wild animals, are enshrined in the second story of the tower gate. Images of 'protector gods' or 'guardian kings' appear at the entrance to the shrine, at the four corners of the altar, in the kitchen and even in the lavatory! The major monasteries often also have a hall dedicated to the founder of that monastery, where an oil lamp is kept burning day and night.

Zen monks are known poetically as *unsui* ('cloud-water'). The aspiring monk is free to choose any monastery, but the process of initiation is intended to test his resolution. On arrival, he prostrates himself and bows three times. He asks permission to enter, but is refused by a senior monk and thrown out. He then sits outside bowing for two days, and only then is allowed inside and accepted into the monastic life.

The Zen monk is allocated one straw tatami mat (about 1 by 2 metres or 3½ by 7 feet) in the zendo, on which he not only sleeps but also meditates and eats. Monastery life revolves around daily zazen practice. This can involve three periods per day, each of around two hours duration. Zazen is preceded by sutra chanting and punctuated by periods of *kinhin*, or walking meditation. One senior monk keeps watch over the others, to make sure they don't fall asleep or fidget. If they do, he may slap their shoulders firmly with a flat bamboo stick called a *keisaku*.

Have the fearless
attitude of a hero
and the loving
heart of a child.

Soyen Shaku

Zen monks are also involved in physical labour (*samu*), such as growing vegetables and rice, building and maintenance, cooking and cleaning. Some teachers advocate longer periods of walking meditation – walking through the woods, even in city streets – in order to bring a meditative awareness to the world outside the zendo. Some Zen monks have made walking a way of life. Known as *komuso*, they wander for years – from temple to temple in search of authentic teachers, to follow the unfolding of the seasons, or for its own sake – before once again settling down.

Other daily activities include sutra chanting, *teisho* or *sanzen* (teachings from the roshi or master), *dokusan* (private interviews between teacher and student), and *takuhatsu* (religious mendicancy – begging for donations). Takuhatsu happens on the third, sixth and eighth days of each month, when the monks walk together to the nearest town and are fed by local people. On the fourth and ninth days of the month, they shave their heads and clean the hondo and the zendo.

At different times during the year, several week-long periods of zazen are scheduled. During these *sesshin* (meaning to 'touch the mind'), monks practise zazen from 3.30 a.m. until 10 p.m., the only interruptions being for short meal and toilet breaks. During this time, no talking, looking around or social greetings are permitted, so that one's full attention is on 'just sitting' or the koan at hand.

In common with other Japanese Buddhists, monks may also be involved in matsuri, religious festivals involving the local community. For instance, the Hana Matsuri ('Flower Festival') on 8 April celebrates the Buddha's birthday by pouring sweet tea over a statue representing the Buddha as a newborn child. The customary anniversaries of the Buddha's enlightenment (8 December) and death (15 February) – or entry into nirvana – are also commemorated.

Zen in the arts

Zen aesthetics

Zen has influenced Japanese culture not only through its religious and political life, but also through the arts. From architecture to cooking, we can speak of a 'Zen aesthetic', characterised by simplicity, refinement, spontaneity and a love of natural forms, textures and lines. Here are some important terms:

- Art works inspired by Zen are expressions of *mushin*, 'no-mind', in which the ordinary separation between the artist, their tools and the works he or she produces disappears. No-mind is also 'beginner's mind' or 'everyday mind': at the end of his arduous training, the master returns to the innocence and spontaneity of the child – and yet is infused with experience and insight.
- *Ri* refers to the true nature of a thing or person, while *ji* is how it takes form. To experience a oneness of action and outcome is to act in accord with ri. To do something that grates against one's inner knowing, or that disadvantages others, is to act *muri*, 'without ri'.
- *Wabi* refers to the tendency of Zen arts to pare things back to their essentials. An object with wabi is restrained, free of adornment.
- *Sabi* refers to objects that have mellowed with age, taking on a melancholy air. Sabi reminds us of the shortness of life and the sadness of its passing.
- *Shibui* refers to something subtle and unstated that manifests itself when all the elements come together in a disciplined but natural and understated way.

A sense of imperfection is also vital to Zen arts. Nature's patterns are always slightly irregular, so if, say, a Zen potter makes a perfect bowl, he or she will mark it, so that it is a truer reflection of life.

Swordsmanship and archery

Zen discipline influenced the relationship between the warrior and his weapons: they were not mere killing tools, but objects imbued with spiritual power.

For instance, the samurai's sword was precious and highly crafted, composed of an inner sandwich of soft metals to give suppleness, and hard metals on the outside for strength, the whole bonded and tempered by heating and cooling at precise temperatures to make it durable and sharp. As for the weapon, so for the warrior, who should be like bamboo: hard on the outside and empty on the inside. The analogies go further: the sword was like the dharma that cuts through all obstacles. It became an extension of the warrior, so that he acted without thought of self or other, life or death.

This looks like sophistry to the Western mind: after all, the object is to kill one's enemy and stay alive! But acting with no-mind, the warrior is able to take advantage of his opponent's weaknesses. A keen student once asked a sword master how long it would take to train. Ten years, was the answer. He then asked how long if he worked diligently day and night. 'In that case, thirty years,' replied the master. He then offered to devote all his energy, his every waking moment, to the task. 'In that case, seventy years,' countered the master. For the first three years, he didn't even touch a sword; he did only manual work. Then the master started creeping up behind him and attacking him with a sword. Only when his senses were sharp enough to react instinctively to every approach did the sword training begin.

As with swords, the technology of Japanese archery differs from its Western counterpart: bows are bigger, the bamboo arrows are lighter and longer, and the bowstring is released using the thumb rather than the index finger.

But the differences go deeper. Where the Western archer aims to hit the bull's eye, the Zen archer aims to forget the target, instead focusing on breath and posture. The course of the arrow, when it finally flies, then reflects the archer's state of mind as much as his or her mastery of technique. To hit the target is akin to resolving a koan.

A disciplined
mind brings
happiness.

Buddha

Architecture and gardens

Zen was a relatively late influence on Japanese architecture. Before it came Shinto shrines, with their use of unpainted, unadorned natural timbers, floors elevated on pillars, thatched roofs, an encircling veranda and intricate handcrafted joinery rather than nails. Later came aristocratic dwellings incorporating Chinese elements, including tiled pagoda-style roofs, clay walls and painted exteriors.

Under the influence of Zen, samurai of the Kamakura period (AD 1185–1333) returned to the simplicity of Shinto design, but with the addition of elements such as *shoji* (rice paper screens to divide the internal space,) and *shoin* (window alcoves with a raised sill overlooking gardens that were used for reading and writing.) Subsequently, movable floor mats were replaced by tatami mats made of woven reeds. The shoin-style dwelling eventually gave way to the more free-form *sukiya*, which continued the tradition of simplicity, openness and naturalness but added elements from the design of teahouses. This became the model for house design.

The lightness and openness of traditional Japanese house and temple design is of benefit in a country prone to earthquakes. The design of Zen temples was also influenced by the need to accommodate Buddhist statues and monks practising zazen. Beyond such practical considerations, the impact of Zen is felt in a preference for simplicity and naturalness, which help create an atmosphere conducive to calming and opening the mind.

Early Japanese garden design also borrowed heavily from the Chinese. In the Heian period (AD 794–1192), the ruling class copied Chinese 'pleasure parks', and in the Kamakura period, wealthy adherents of the Pure Land sect modelled their gardens on their fantasies of the Western Paradise of Amida Buddha. But the preference of Sung dynasty (AD 960–1279) landscape painters in China for empty space, vast vistas and minute human figures also crept into Japanese gardens; under the influence of Zen, gardens became more meditative and less crowded.

The gardens in Zen temples are three-dimensional equivalents of landscape paintings, and employ some of the same conventions, such as perspective and foreshortening. They also use visual and psychological tricks to create the illusions of space and distance, such as creating narrowing streams and placing bonsai plants in the background, or carefully placing boulders so as to suggest mountains.

At the same time, great care is taken to create the appearance of naturalness and age. For instance, a wall that has been stained with water may not be repainted, while a rock that has acquired a patina of moss is all the more valued. And temple gardens are not cut off from the world around them, with *sakura* (cherry blossom) flowers in spring giving way to beds of rusty leaves in fall, and even a blanket of snow in winter.

The gardens most characteristic of Zen are the *kare sansui*, or dry landscapes, which employ flat beds of raked sand punctuated by islands of stone to create an atmosphere reminiscent of Sung dynasty landscape paintings. They often open out from temple verandas, and are designed primarily as objects of meditation, their austereness intended to help empty the mind of clutter and cares.

Ryoanji

The most famous dry Zen garden is in the temple of Ryoanji in Kyoto. Built around AD 1490, it is a long, rectangular courtyard of rippled sand with five groups of stones set asymmetrically in mossy ground – fifteen stones in all. It is what is missing that makes Ryoanji great. The viewer cannot see all fifteen stones simultaneously. This has been interpreted as symbolic of the nature of reality, which cannot be grasped in its entirety all at once. Other layers of interpretation have been suggested, from the likeness of the garden to islands in the ocean to the relationship between the stones and the sand being like that between form and emptiness in Mahayana doctrine. But like Zen itself, the garden transcends all attempts at interpretation, to be just itself. It is a 'mirror for the mind': what each visitor sees in it is a reflection of his or her own mind.

Painting and calligraphy

Early Japanese landscape painting was much influenced by its Sung dynasty equivalent in China, with its preference for monochromes, empty space, and vast, 'cloud-hidden' mountainous and forested landscapes in which human figures were relatively insignificant.

By the time a painting academy was established at the Shokokuji temple in Kyoto, Zen themes began to appear. A famous early example is *Catching a Catfish with a Gourd*, by Josetsu, the head of the academy, who was active in the period AD 1400–13. A man stands by a river, a gourd in his outstretched hands, hoping to catch the catfish swimming past him. This painting is thought to be a parable for the difficulty of grasping enlightenment, which is as slippery as a catfish.

After Josetsu came Sesshu (AD 1420–1506), a Zen monk who travelled to China and came back to set up a studio in a seaside village. He is renowned for developing the techniques known as *shin*, featuring bold, earthy lines and sharp angles, and *so*, which uses blurred streaks and ink washes to blend elements of the landscape that the shin style would make distinct. No matter the painter or the style, Zen paintings seek to transcend mere beauty and manifest an unspoken truth, placing humans in their true relationship to nature and the cosmos.

Japanese calligraphy (*sumi-e*), which often appears on landscape paintings and portraits but is an art form in its own right, is similarly infused with Zen doctrines and discipline. Originally a sign of literacy, and thus of social class, calligraphy became a more aesthetic pursuit following the invention of the fifty-character syllabary in the early Heian period. Less complex than Chinese characters, it was more conducive to artistic flourishes.

Calligraphers use an ink block called *sumi*, made of lamp black and glue, a brush of natural animal hair, an ink stone to grind and wet the ink, and paper or silk as a writing surface. Because there is no room for mistakes with ink, sumi-e reflects the calligrapher's state of mind, and experts can easily tell the work of a master who is not only technically proficient but spontaneous and breathtaking.

Poetry

Early Japanese poetry also shows strong Chinese influences. Nevertheless, even the first anthology of Japanese poetry, the *Man'yōshū* (compiled in the eighth century), shows both the form and the concerns that would shape later haiku poetry. As well as longer verses on heroic themes, called *choka*, there are five-line, thirty-two-syllable verses known as *waka*, which reflect the characteristic Japanese concern for the passing of beauty and of life.

Waka about the passing of both the seasons and love dominate the next great anthology, the twelfth century *Kokinshū*. The next form to emerge was the renga, consisting of linked waka by different poets. Both forms stagnated under the burden of rules about what subjects should be written about, and in what order. By the sixteenth century the style now known as *haiku* – seventeen syllables in lines of five, seven and five syllables, usually including a 'season word' – emerged. Originally the first verse of a renga, haiku too began to rigidify, until Matsuo Basho (AD 1644–1694) emerged to reinvigorate it.

Haiku is quintessentially Zen in its bare simplicity, its preference for nature over culture, its awareness of impermanence – tinged with *sabi*, melancholy – and its insistence on the oneness of the ordinary and sacred worlds. ('Achieve enlightenment, then return to this world of ordinary humanity,' advised Basho.) On one level, haiku are descriptions of actual events, but they also point to deeper truths and (like koans) burst the mind out of its habitual ways of perceiving things.

Later haiku masters such as Buson (AD 1716–1783) and Issa (AD 1763–1827) were less thoroughly steeped in Zen teachings than Basho, but Zen qualities so permeated the haiku form that they did not need to be. Today, haiku is practised in Japan and around the world by many people – people who are, in effect, practising Zen without knowing it.

Basho

Basho (meaning 'plantain leaves') is a pseudonym for Matsuo Manefusa (AD 1644–94). Born into a samurai family at a time when their power had waned, and put into the service of a *daimyo* (feudal lord) who died when Basho was 22, he travelled first to Kyoto to study haiku, and then to Edo (Tokyo) to teach and write. His early verses are technically competent, but he later took up Zen practice and travelled extensively, giving his haiku a greater depth of feeling and flashes of satori:

> *An old pond*
> *A frog jumps in*
> *Plop!*

This is Basho's most famous haiku, but he is also famous for *Oku no Hosomichi* (Narrow Road to the Far North). Ostensibly the record of a long and difficult journey he took north and west of Edo in 1689, it blends genres: fact and fiction, and prose and poetry of different styles. Here is the first verse, which he composed on the day of his departure:

Spring is passing by!
Birds are weeping and the eyes
Of fish fill with tears.
—Matsuo Bashō,
  The Narrow Road to Oku, Tokyo, 1996, p. 23 (Translation: Donald Keene)

Just before his death in November 1694, he wrote his last haiku:

Sick on a journey,
my dreams wander
the withered fields.
(Translation: Robert Hass)

The 'journey' is that of poetry, of Zen practice, and of life itself.

Flower arranging

The ancient Japanese believed that such beautiful things as flowers must have spiritual power, so began cutting stems to have them indoors. Flowers were used to mark sites at which to welcome the gods. Today, a decoration of pine, bamboo, and plum blossoms called *kadomatsu* is often displayed at the front door of Japanese houses to welcome the new year. *Ikebana* (flower arranging) is also said to have developed out of the Buddhist ritual of offering flowers to spirits of the dead.

The principles and practices of early ikebana were passed on by a group of priests called the Ikenobo – named after the *ike no bu* or 'hut by the pond' in Kyoto where Senno, the founder of this school, lived out his retirement in the sixteenth century. This style, called *tatebana* or *rikka*, involved complex, mandala-like representations of the world. The influence of Zen was evident in a preference for asymmetrical arrangements and as natural an appearance as possible – in spite of there being numerous rules and symbolic functions for each of the three main branches (representing heaven, man and Earth) and the four supporting branches.

A more Zen-like style, known as *chabana* or *nageire*, which stressed simplicity and spontaneity, emerged with the tea master Sen no Rikyu (AD 1521–1591). Instead of complex seven-part designs, one or two blossoms might be placed in a pot in a way that was designed to look casual. Too austere for the average Japanese household, a compromise style called *seika* or *shoka* emerged in the eighteenth century. This style was characterised by a tight bundle of stems forming a triangular three-branched asymmetrical structure.

Today, there are various schools, including *ohahra*, which uses Western flowers and trays called *suiban*, and *sogetsu*, which adheres to traditional design principles but uses modern materials such as scrap metal. The most radical style is *jiyuka*, or 'free flowers', in which arrangements reflect the artist's emotions and ideas rather than natural beauty. Ikebana is one of the arts taught to young Japanese women of marrying age, and it is now practised around the world. The Zen influence remains in the idea that arranging flowers is a means of contemplation, a meditation on the relationship between nature and the Self.

Food

Japanese food is often criticised for being bland (the hot green paste wasabi notwithstanding!). But it is truer to say that the Japanese regard taste as no more important than texture, colour, smell, the way food is arranged, and even the quality of the ceramics or lacquerware on which it is served. The overall effect is to engage all the senses: surely a more satisfying experience than an assault on the taste buds that leaves the stomach reeling and the soul untouched. This applies even to the humble bento lunch-box, the Western equivalent of which, the TV dinner, is sad and crude by comparison.

This is without even mentioning the highly ritualised nature of Japanese dining, which begins with the offering *itadakimasu* ('I gratefully receive') and ends with *gochisosamadeshita* ('Thank you for the treat'). Both are blessings, ways of recognising that the lives of animals and plants have been sacrificed in order to feed us, and that eating is a social and even sacred act.

The ingredients, aesthetics and rituals of Japanese cuisine all bear the marks of Buddhism, especially Zen. In fact, the consumption of meat and even fish was prohibited by a vegetarian ordinance between AD 676 and AD 737, under the rule of devout Buddhist emperors. Fish and shellfish were allowed in AD 737, and the eating of meat became common only during the Meiji Restoration (AD 1868–1912).

The characteristic Buddhist style of Japanese cooking is shojin-ryori, a combination of words meaning religious asceticism and cooking. The use of seasonal vegetables and wild plants from the mountains, served with seaweed, fresh or dried tofu, and nuts and seeds, goes beyond the dictates of taste and health, becoming an aid to enlightenment.

Shojin-ryori is derived from the food served to Zen monks — usually rice, vegetables and a side dish — and avoids meat on the basis that killing animals is a violation of the Buddhist precepts. It is said to have been introduced by monks from China in the thirteenth century. Such a diet is said to aid clarity of mind. (For this reason even mildly spicy foods such as onion and garlic are avoided.) In Zen temples, monks and students eat very fast (by Western standards) in order to not become attached to food.

Even kaiseki, the most elegant and expensive form of Japanese cuisine today, has Buddhist origins: *kai* are the folds of kimonos, inside which monks traditionally placed heated stones (*seki*) to keep out the cold as they meditated and slept in unheated temple halls.

Tea ceremony

Chazen ichimi (Zen and tea are one)
— Traditional Japanese saying

There is an old Zen legend that has the first tea bush sprouting from the ground where Bodhidharma, angry with himself for having fallen asleep while meditating, threw his eyelashes after tearing them off.

Tea was already being drunk in China by the time of Confucius (around 500 BC). However, it wasn't always prepared with infusions of the leaves of the tea plant. In Tang dynasty China (AD 618–907), and in Russia, the leaves were smoked and dried into a cake – often with other ingredients, such as salt, ginger and orange peel – before being boiled. In the Sung dynasty (AD 960–1279) the practice began of whipping finely ground leaves in boiling water, creating a frothy brew that was bright green if fresh leaves were used. This, rather than the later practice of steeping the leaves in boiled water, became the basis of the Japanese tea ceremony.

Cha-no-yu (tea ceremony), or *chado*, developed when the aristocratic use of tea drinking as a refined entertainment came together with the ritualised drinking of tea by Zen monks to stay awake and as a religious sacrament. It gained its familiar form in the sixteenth century under the influence of Sen no Rikyu (AD 1521–1591), who defined the requirements for the ceremony as harmony, tranquillity, purity and respect.

Tea is taken in a small, rustic-looking thatched-roof hut called a *cha-shitu*. As with the pottery and implements used in the ceremony, the materials used in the teahouse are intended to give the impression of poverty, but they are actually highly refined and expensive.

Guests are met at the gate by the host of the house, and escorted along the *roji*, or 'dewy path', through a simple garden. Placed on the path are a stone water basin and bamboo dipper for rinsing one's mouth, and a stone lantern. Entry is not by a doorway, but by a square hole through which visitors crawl, ensuring that they leave behind their sense of self-importance. Shoes and weapons are left outside. Inside, incense is burning and a kettle is heating over the fire. The interior of the house is adorned only by a calligraphic scroll (*kakemono*), a flower arrangement and the tea bowl, each of which guests admire before sitting down. The host may serve a light meal before the tea ceremony begins.

The host rinses and dries the tea bowl *(chawan)*. A bamboo scoop is used to put powdered *koicha* (green tea) into the bowl. Boiling water is then added with a bamboo dipper, and the host mixes the ingredients with precise movements. The bowl is offered to the guest of honour, who takes three sips of the bitter, frothy mix and wipes the lip before handing it to the next guest. When all have drunk and the tea is finished, the host rinses the bowl and makes a second, lighter brew known as *usucha*. After this has been finished, the guests relax and are given a bowl of sweets. They are free to comment on the garden, the tea or the tea bowl, which is a work of art in itself.

Cha-no-yu brings together the Zen approach to architecture, gardens, flower arrangement, calligraphy and ceramic art, and is therefore considered by many to be the epitome of Zen culture. It combines sabi, the melancholic awareness of the passing of time, with wabi, a restrained simplicity of form. Together, these elements create an atmosphere that can at once quiet the anxious mind and – by its careful attention to detail and to ritual – help the warrior develop mental discipline.

"

Have good trust in
yourself … not in the
One that you think you
should be, but in the
One that you are.

"

Maezumi Roshi

Zen in the West

Introduction

Zen was formally introduced to the West when Soto master Soyen Shaku addressed the first World Parliament of Religions in Chicago in 1893. However, inklings of Zen can be found in older European literature, art and philosophy. For instance, when the English artist and poet William Blake wrote in the following poem, 'Auguries of Innocence':

> *To see a World in a Grain of Sand,*
> *And a heaven in a Wild Flower,*
> *Hold Infinity in the palm of your hand*
> *And Eternity in an hour*

he was expressing something of the Zen recognition of the sublime in the everyday.

Inklings or analogies there may have been, but Zen also represented a challenge to the Western mindset, and much energy has been expended over the past fifty years or so in making it comprehensible to Westerners. During this time it has had a profound impact, not only through giving spiritual direction to a generation of seekers disillusioned with the monotheistic traditions of the West and the materialism of modern culture, but also more broadly, in areas as diverse as the arts and psychotherapy. Zen has itself been transformed in the process, with the emergence of female and lay (non-celibate) teachers, wilderness sesshins and Zen psychotherapy, among other developments. The changes are so extensive that it has been suggested that a new koan should be added to the Rinzai canon: 'When is Zen, Zen?'

After a boom in interest in the 1960s and 1970s among 'baby boomers', Zen has settled into a more mature but less obvious presence in the West. In the meantime, the Theravada tradition, represented by various Vipassana teachers, and the Vajrayana teachings of the Tibetan schools, led by the Dalai Lama, have been gradually gaining in popularity and acceptance. It remains to be seen whether Western Buddhism amounts to a fourth 'turning of the wheel', or will be regarded as an adaptation of these first three traditions.

There has also been cross-fertilisation with the contemplative dimension of Christianity, so that some now speak of 'Zen Christianity', with practices such as meditation on the image of God and prayer as a chant or mantra.

Some major figures

One of Soyen Shaku's students was the scholar D.T. Suzuki (1870–1966). While not himself a roshi, he had a deep understanding of the Rinzai tradition in particular. In lectures in America and Europe and in books such as the three-volume classic, *Essays in Zen Buddhism*, he introduced a generation of Westerners to Zen thought in the 1950s and 1960s. Calling himself 'a Japanese aspiring to world citizenship', he married an American and lived in the USA for a quarter of a century. Along with his contemporaries in the Kyoto School of Japanese philosophy, he emphasised those aspects of Zen most foreign to Western thinking, such as emptiness and satori, and paid little attention to ethics or the role of karma. Late in life he was asked if he thought about the afterlife. He replied, 'Yes, but what about here and now? Would it not be too late after death?'

A very different Japanese person also influential in the transmission of Zen to the West was the Soto master Shunryu Suzuki (1904–1971), who set up, in California, the first Zen training monastery outside Asia, and whose informal talks on Zen meditation and practice have been compiled into a beautifully clear, profound book.

Of course the traffic was two-way, and especially after World War II, a number of Americans and Europeans made their way to Japan to steep themselves in Zen. One was Robert Aitken (1919–2010), who was captured during the war – he was a civilian – in Guam, and introduced to Zen in a Japanese prison camp. He returned to Japan after the war, became friends with D.T. Suzuki, and trained in a Soto school that uses koan practice. In 1959 he and his wife Anne established the Diamond Sangha in Hawaii. He was given the title Roshi in 1974, and has been instrumental in the greater focus of Western Zen on ethical and political issues.

Another important figure was Philip Kapleau (1912–2004) (also later Roshi). Kapleau trained in Japan with Yasutani Roshi and set up the Rochester Zen Center in 1966. The first part of *The Three Pillars of Zen* (1965) is devoted to Yasutani's instructions for beginning students, and is still considered an important source of Zen teachings. He has also written on the friction between the emerging North American Zen and Japanese traditionalists, and on how Zen can help us face illness, pain and death.

There have also been Zen teachers from Korea (e.g. Seung Sahn (1927–2004)) and Vietnam (Thich Nhat Hanh) who have established centres and lineages in America and Europe and written books in English to bring their versions of Zen to a wider audience.

Issues in Western Zen

In adapting to the West, Zen has had to face a number of important issues. Some changes, such as the emergence of female teachers, have been made with relatively little controversy. Other issues have been more difficult: who could call themselves a Roshi; how to financially support zendos and teachers; how much zazen and rituals should be adapted to make them easier or more relevant; and what to do about the numerous instances of sexual and financial misconduct by teachers of both Japanese and Western origin.

This last issue has caused considerable debate about the relationship of satori to ethical conduct. It has been difficult for many Westerners to accept that a teacher who has experienced a measure of enlightenment and has been given authority to teach can violate the moral codes and laws of the wider society. Followers are sometimes tempted to condone such misconduct on the grounds that the same rules do not apply to the enlightened as to the unenlightened, or that upsetting conventional morality is one way teachers bring their students to insight.

Still, tolerance for unethical conduct is decreasing. Sometimes in tandem with their Tibetan and Theravadan brethren, Zen teachers and students have taken strong stands on feminist, environmental, human and animal rights and anti-war issues. These stands reflect the Ten Grave Precepts of Mahayana Buddhism. The Western Zen approach to political and ethical issues is characterised by a commitment to equanimity (not being drawn into negative emotions), self-awareness (as Thich Nhat Hanh says, 'Don't just do something, sit there!'), and non-violent resistance.

Beat Zen

New York novelist Jack Kerouac started meditating after reading Ashvaghosha's *Life of the Buddha*, and wrote in his notebook that as he meditated he saw 'golden swarms of nothing'. In his famous 1956 novel *Dharma Bums*, he has Japhy Ryder (a pseudonym for Zen poet and teacher Gary Snyder) predict a future in which the visions of poets would revolutionise the country.

Beat Zen was part of the Beat Generation, the name given to a movement that emerged in the 1950s combining elements of jazz, Buddhism and youth rebellion. Actually, there wasn't much Zen (in the traditional sense) in it. Kerouac, Allen Ginsberg, Snyder, Alan Watts and Kenneth Rexroth took the spontaneity, direct insight and formlessness of Zen as their hallmark, largely forgetting about the rigid discipline, hierarchy and conformity of Japanese Zen.

Still, each of these writers studied and practised Buddhism. Snyder went to Japan in 1956 to begin twelve years of 'real Zen study', and later taught Zen (as well as poetry and environmental activism) from his zendo home in northern California, on college campuses and through his books.

Watts was originally an Episcopalian priest, and then taught at the Academy of Asian Studies in San Francisco. He had a radio show in Berkeley from 1954 and later in Los Angeles, called 'Way Beyond the West', in which he introduced listeners to Asian spiritual traditions as 'a cure for education and culture'. He wrote *The Way of Zen* in 1956, and *Beat Zen, Square Zen, and Zen*, which saw him tagged as the 'father of the hippies', in 1959.

> *Robert Wilson: What is Zen?*
> *Alan Watts: [Soft chuckling.]*
> *Robert Wilson: Would you care to enlarge on that?*
> *Alan Watts: [Loud laughing.]*

The original Beats, Watts said, were young veterans who rejected the materialistic, conformist life they found on their return from the war and instead hitchhiked around the USA or travelled overseas in search of spiritual wisdom. They were the forebears of the 1960s counterculture that gave rise to the anti-war, feminist and environmental movements, and Zen gave them a language for their rebellion and their spiritual hunger.

Zen and psychotherapy

Practising Zazen has been found to reduce anxiety and depression, allow coping strategies to work better, and increase feelings of well-being. However, there are many kinds of meditation, which work in different ways. Yogis who meditate with closed eyes are oblivious to the external world, while Zen meditators (who keep their eyes slightly open) become keenly attuned to the environment. Relaxation isn't the only goal; grappling with a riddle or puzzle (koan), for instance, is likely to increase anxiety at times.

Given the impact of meditation on human behaviour, and the aim of all Buddhist thought and practice – to increase happiness – it is not surprising that for over fifty years a fruitful dialogue has existed between Zen and Western psychotherapies. At first glance, the detachment and discipline of Zen, which help us to 'get out of our own way', seem to have little in common with the process of delving into our emotional life and family issues to resolve personal problems. As the Freudian Erich Fromm put it, 'psychoanalysis is a therapy for mental illness; Zen is a way to spiritual salvation'. Or as Zen teacher Bon Soeng puts it:

> … in Zen meditation we're not really trying to explore something, we're working with 'don't know mind' and letting everything be.

Still, both Zen and psychotherapy work with the mind – and often the body and soul, too – to transform suffering into happiness, so there are commonalities. The cross-fertilisation has probably been strongest in transpersonal psychology, which aims to integrate psychotherapies with spiritual traditions by seeing them as relating to different stages in the evolution of consciousness. Zen practice also has much in common with existential and gestalt therapies, which are more focused on the body and present reality than on the distant past and repressed memories and traumas. We can only really live in the present, and if Zen can help us to be fully present with each breath, then this is good therapy.

Conversely, many Western Zen teachers now have psychological or psychotherapeutic training, which enables them to understand the emotional problems that arise for students in Zen practice – for instance, in regard to sexuality and relationships. The best of them recognise that the insights offered by Zen practice are meaningless unless one is already grounded in everyday reality. So Zen complements psychotherapy, rather than being a substitute for it.

The Buddha on solving problems
The classical Buddhist attitude towards understanding psychological problems is illustrated by the analogy the Buddha drew with a man whose hand had been pierced by a poisoned arrow, but who refused to have the arrow pulled out until he knew all about the person who shot it.

Truly, such a man would die before he could adequately learn all this. Therefore, the man who seeks his own welfare should pull out this arrow – this arrow of lamentation, pain, and sorrow.

So it's less important to understand how our suffering came about than to do what we can in the present to end it.

Zen and Western culture

In the West, Zen has not only been practised in meditation halls. The Zen arts have all become established in Western culture, and in each case, Westerners have reached the highest levels of attainment. There are also practices that derive from Zen but have been adapted to Western minds and bodies, such as macrobiotics and shiatsu. Zen aesthetics have influenced European and American designers in the visual arts (think minimalism and formlessness in abstract art), architecture (clean lines, uncluttered spaces, and natural materials) and landscape design (pebble gardens, feature rocks and bonsai).

The written word bears the strongest mark of Zen. From books like this one that deal directly with Zen, to others that put Zen in the title to emphasise their reflective or spiritual qualities (*Zen and the Art of Making a Living*, *Zen and the Guitar*, and so on), hundreds of 'Zen' books are now available in English. Then there is the way Zen has inspired novelists, from the mynah birds that cry 'Attention!' in Aldous Huxley's *Island* to Robert Pirsig's hippy classic *Zen and the Art of Motorcycle Maintenance*, which has the author tuned in, Zen-like, to his motorcycle as he rides across the States.

Zen has come to signify a spare, rustic aesthetic, liberation from form and tradition, and a life of spontaneity. Yet much of this Western appropriation of Zen is ironic, in view of its history in Japan of being highly disciplined, even militaristic.

The turn of the twenty-first century witnessed a new development: designer Zen. A designer sees her clothes as symbols of a lifestyle she calls Zen, and wearers are reminded to 'Be present, not Tense'. '24/7', 'streamlined', and 'vision' are other buzz-words. Journalist Janelle Brown calls such lifestyle products 'Zen Lite ... a romanticising of the cultural aesthetics of Japanese monks without requiring the sacrifice'.

Her cynicism is well-founded, but a sense of humour has always been a part of Zen, too. And as many a writer reminds us (to paraphrase a famous Taoist saying), the Zen that can be described – let alone the Zen that can be ripped off – is not the real Zen.

Living the Zen life

How to practise zazen

The best way to understand Zen is by practising zazen. Whether your aim is to live what you have read in books like this one, to reduce stress, to be more self-aware or to achieve enlightenment, the best place to practise zazen is in a Zen centre. There are Zen centres in most major cities. If there isn't one near where you live, or if you prefer to practise on your own, here are some tips to get you started.

- Find a place that is quiet but uncluttered (and light: sleep is not the same as meditation!). It is good to be close to the ground, on a surface that is neither too soft to be supportive, nor too hard to be comfortable.
- Try to sit at a time of day when you can take time out but are likely to still feel fresh.
- Wear clothes that are loose and comfortable.
- Posture: try sitting with your bottom on a cushion (*zafu*) about six inches high in full or half-lotus position (one or both feet folded over the other leg) with your back almost straight, but not rigid. Usually it is most comfortable if the lower spine curves slightly to the front. If this is not comfortable, try sitting on a low bench with your knees together in front of you and your feet tucked under the bench, or even sitting up straight in a supportive chair – but remember that the more contained your body is, the more focused your concentration is likely to be.
- Hands: put one palm on the other on your lap, a few inches below your navel. The traditional *mudra*, or hand gesture, for Zen meditation has one hand resting on the other with palms upward and thumbs touching.
- Tilt your head slightly forward and keep your eyes half-open, so that they are focused on a point on the ground about a yard in front of you.
- Breathing: some teachers advocate a totally natural process, while others have students take a short in-breath and a longer out-breath. Either way, as the mind quietens, breathing will also naturally slow down. With each in-breath, we take in new life; with each out-breath, we let go of whatever we have been holding inside.

Having got started, here are some hints about how to proceed:

- If it helps you concentrate, count your breaths from one to ten, then start again – but if you're a highly disciplined, obsessive type, this can become a fixation, so beware!
- Allow thoughts, feelings, memories and fantasies to arise and naturally pass away, rather than hanging on to them.
- When your attention wanders, don't beat yourself up about it; just bring your attention back to your breath.
- If sounds intrude from the outside world, don't try to shut them out, but allow them to enter and leave your body and mind with each breath.
- Feel your centre of consciousness naturally sink gradually from your head into your *hara*, or gut.
- If you keep dozing off, maybe you need rest more than meditation!
- Pain can be a useful teacher, so imagine your breath going to the painful part of your body, then try to breathe through it rather than pushing it away. However, it isn't good to deny the body, so if pain persists, move to a more comfortable position, even if this means using back support.
- As your practice deepens, you may notice your psychic powers becoming more acute, and wonderful or terrible fantasies, called *makkyo*, take hold of your mind. These are diversions, so see if you can let them go.
- Develop a simple ritual to end zazen, like a simple *gassho* (hands together and upright at heart level, with a short bow forward) or ringing a bell, then get up and get on with other things without mulling over zazen.
- Start by sitting for a short period – around ten minutes – and gradually build it up. Like anything worth doing, meditation takes practice to do well, but quality is more important than quantity.

If you follow these simple steps, the world you see – after even a short period of zazen – will not be the same as the one you saw beforehand.

In a monastery or temple, zazen is accompanied by much ritual and discipline. The atmosphere of group practice, with sutra chanting, *kinhin* (walking meditation) and *teisho* (teachings), is thought to deepen one's practice. However, you can still benefit by doing zazen at home – if necessary, even sitting up in bed with pillows to support your back, or in the bath! Attitude and intent are more important than the form they take. Above all, be kind to yourself.

Living in the here and now

It is one thing to feel calm and centred when meditating, but another to bring this awareness into a life of blaring televisions, fighting kids, looming appointments and housework that won't do itself. Where is Zen, then?

The effects of regular meditation are felt quite naturally in daily life. We learn not to react so quickly to things that would normally upset us. We can witness the chaos around us and even inside us without buying into it.

We can also consciously bring a little Zen into everyday life. When we feel ourselves getting stressed, angry or upset, instead of just giving in to the emotion, we can step back from it, take time out to acknowledge our feelings, and practise deep breathing to return consciousness to the body.

Beyond this, walking to work, exercising, gardening and other forms of work that don't heavily engage the mind can become extensions of zazen, by paying close attention to our actions and environment and returning to the breath when we notice we are 'elsewhere'.

Even work that demands most of our attention can have a Zen quality if we approach it with mindfulness. We can remind ourselves to stay with what is, rather than acting on the basis of 'pie in the sky' fantasies or often unconscious worse-case scenarios. Every Zen student is a bodhisattva-in-waiting, with a commitment to treating others (and themselves) with respect and compassion. So, we can ask ourselves what the impact of our actions will be, not just on our bank balance or health, but on the people with whom we work, the environment, and the many beings involved in giving life to, and creating, the things that we consume.

Ultimately, this means living each moment to the full, as if we might die not even tomorrow but in the blink of an eye. We might reflect on a koan of our own making, such as 'What is the source of my life?' This is quite different from deciding to 'just do it' as if we should indulge every passion or impulse and damn the consequences. It is an invitation to bridge the gap between now and forever.

It's only natural

Zen inherited from Taoism and Shinto a reverence for nature that goes beyond a spare, rustic aesthetic and a love of mountains as retreats from the world. In Zen, the contemplation of nature bridges the usual divide between human subjectivity and the external world, becoming a study of our own nature.

Reverence for nature begins with paying close attention to the life around us: the bugs and lizards that crawl in the back door, the sweet smell of cut grass, the morning dew. It also means noticing the big picture: how our actions have an impact on the world around us. Through the writings of Robert Aitken and Gary Snyder, Zen has been influential in the Deep Ecology movement, which is founded on the idea that humans are part of nature, 'plain members of the biotic community', rather than its stewards or overlords. This could be a purely intellectual or moralistic attitude, except that the more we pay attention to the world around us, the less separate we feel from it.

One of Dogen's most beautiful works is the *Sansuikyo*, or Mountains and Rivers Sutra. In it, he uses poetic language to break through our separateness from nature:

> *All waters appear at the foot of the eastern mountains. Above all waters are all mountains. Walking beyond and walking within are both done on water. All mountains walk with their toes on all waters and splash there.*

This doesn't seem to make sense, but that doesn't mean it isn't true. Try it. When you are walking, feel the pavement walk with you, maybe even call to you, tell you a story.

On the Zen path, things can get a bit weird at times. In the beginning, trees are just trees, mountains just mountains. Later, they lose their familiar forms as we see beneath surfaces. Then, finally, 'Trees are trees again and mountains are again mountains,' as we are grounded more fully in everyday life. In a sense (and unlike most Western psychotherapies), Zen encourages what Plato called 'the unexamined life'. Instead of questioning everything, looking for signs and portents, checking and rechecking our motivations and reactions, we become innocents again, doing what needs to be done in the moment.

When hungry, I eat.
When tired, I sleep.

This is reverence for nature.

Dealing with pain and death

In life, there's one kind of happiness that comes from avoiding everything unpleasant and painful as much as we can. This usually doesn't work for very long. Then there's another kind that comes from accepting whatever comes our way with equanimity, as if offering a deep bow for whatever the gods or fate or blind luck has thrown our way.

This is the Zen way, and it starts with the breath. With each in-breath, we take in all life, and with each out-breath, we let it pass away. It sounds straightforward, but even in zazen, we are often faced with difficult emotions, memories and fantasies. Just breathing through them reminds us that our imagination is the root of much suffering (and of much bliss, too), and that if we can let it in, it will also pass away.

Physical pain arises often in zazen. It is easy to become engulfed by it, or to put a lot of energy into pushing it away. If we keep returning to the breath or the koan and imagine our breath going to that part of the body, we feel its ebbs and flows. This tends to make it feel more like a process in which we are involved than something external that we must either suffer through or conquer with willpower or drugs.

The same goes for emotional and existential pain: the pain of being alive in a world that sometimes seems cold, hard, loveless and meaningless. These feelings are real enough at the time, and zazen can help by providing a sense of stability and grounding. We can turn our dilemma into a spiritual practice, for instance, by reflecting on a koan of our own making. But Zen isn't everything, and there is no shame in knowing when to seek outside help.

When master Hofaku realised he was dying, he called his monks together and said:
'This last week my energy has been draining – no cause for worry. It is just that death is near.'
'You are about to die! What does it mean?' asked one of the monks.
'We will go on living. And what does that mean?'
'They are both the way of things,' Hofaku replied.
'But how can I understand two such different states?'
'When it rains it pours,' he answered, and calmly died.

While other Buddhist traditions teach the doctrine of reincarnation, Zen avoids speculating on life after death, in the belief that how one lives is far more important.

When death comes, the task is to face it with equanimity, whether we are the one dying or it is someone close to us. This doesn't mean detaching from feelings, however, as a story told by Kapleau about Soyen Shaku illustrates. When he was on his morning walk with his attendant and heard wailing from a house, Soyen Shaku went inside and asked,

'Why is everyone crying?' He was told, 'We are mourning the death of our child.' Immediately the abbot took a seat among the family and began loudly weeping and wailing with them. On the way back to the temple the attendant asked the master, 'Do you know these people?' 'No,' replied the abbot. 'Then why did you cry with them?' 'To share their sorrow,' responded the abbot.

While the ideal is to face death with equanimity, the reality is that death often brings out intense feelings of grief and anger – or denial. As this story illustrates, from a Zen perspective, we can give ourselves permission to fully feel the range of our emotions surrounding death. Frequently, a peaceful death happens only at the end of a long process of coming to terms with all our feelings about it. Then, we can let go.

Zen and the art of helping

Helping others is the role of the bodhisattva-in-waiting. Zen emphasises that working on oneself is the best way to help others. As spiritual teacher Ram Dass puts it, 'All you have to give to another person is your own being.' Chaos theory tells us that a butterfly flapping its wings in the Amazon can start a hurricane in North America. How much more influential on the karma of the world, then, is a person who spends hours or decades in solitary meditation, whether on a mountaintop in the Himalayas or in a suburban living room!

If we don't do inner work or spiritual practice, we are likely to use our engagement with others as a way of fulfilling our need for recognition. We might even seek out people with particular problems in order to work out our own 'stuff'. As Frank Ostaseski, who founded the Zen Hospice Project in San Francisco, puts it, 'I thought if I was with someone whose pain was worse than mine, mine might not be so bad.'

At the other extreme, if we decide that we can't help anyone else until we have sorted ourselves out, we are likely to navel-gaze until we die. Here is a koan for such situations:

The world is burning up. What am I not to do?

Practising zazen can assist helpers to take time out and relax, reducing the risk of burnout. But it can go deeper. We can ask ourselves, who is really helping whom here? Stepping away from the role of the helper, we can learn from those supposedly being helped. This is true compassion, which means 'suffering with'. We help others best when we suffer with them, and this means being open to our own suffering. Then, we can also see beyond the outer form – the patient dying of cancer, the elderly parent angry at their loss of mobility, the homeless beggar – to the loving, hurting fellow human being beneath. In truth, we are probably just as scared, lonely, confused and pained as they are.

The art of helping is a lot about surrender. Often, when we want to reach out and help another person, we already have an idea about how they should be: 'Get a job!' 'Why do you go back to him/her?' We can only know what it's like for someone else when we've walked a mile in their shoes – after which we're much less likely to judge. Our role as helper-bodhisattvas is to listen, support and point to the goodness in others without denying their pain. If we do feel the need to intervene with 'tough love', we need to be very clear for whom we're doing it.

When you reach the top of the mountain, keep climbing.

Zen Koan

Zen stink, Zen laughter

Religions and their followers tend to take themselves too seriously. After all, killing someone because they don't agree with you is not very enlightened, is it? 'The stink of Zen' is what seeps out of people who are so intent on diligently following their practice and striving for enlightenment that they imagine they are better than others. A master once complained to his students, 'All this talk about Zen is making me sick to my stomach!'

Zen masters are famous for puncturing their students' pomposity and impudence with nonsensical answers, insults, slaps, even body blows. In the modern West, such behaviour is frowned on, but family and friends are usually good at reminding us when we stink of Zen. Even better, Zen undermines itself in many ways, from its paradoxical use of language and rejection of book learning to its use of humour as an aid in practice. Here are some modern Zen jokes (some of which also stink), collected by Craig Presson:

Q: What did the Zen monk say to the hot dog vendor?
A: Make me one with everything!
Q: What did the Zen monk REALLY say to the hot dog vendor?

Q: How many Zen students does it take to change a light bulb?
A: Two. One to change it and one not to.

Q: How many Zen masters does it take to change a light bulb?
A: Tree in the golden forest.

Q: Why don't Buddhists vacuum in corners?
A: Because they have no attachments.

Inconclusion

Zen is a 'finger pointing to the moon': when one has seen the moon, the finger can be forgotten. So, too, with this book. I hope it has opened up the world of Zen to you, explaining its history and doctrines, its practices and influences. At the same time, it should leave you feeling a little confused. Zen has no easy answers: that would be an insult to your intelligence and to the wondrous complexity of the world in which we live.

Having read this book, you can best understand more of Zen by practising it, in whatever way seems appropriate.

If that leads into what Zen calls the 'great doubt', where everything you cherished as true and real is called into question, then so be it. You can always drop it and go back to your old life. If it leads away from doubt and despair and into a stronger sense of your value as one precious, irreplaceable human being among seven-and-a-half billion others, then that's good too.

Either way, never forget that others are out there wandering along the same road. That includes all the buddhas and bodhisattvas of past and future generations – teachers all, whether they take the form of a stupid boss, or needy kids or that fly buzzing in your face while you try to meditate.

Oh, and the 'essence of Zen'? There is no essence of Zen. That is the essence of Zen.